Down to Earth
at Walden

Down to Earth at Walden

Written and Illustrated by
MARILYNNE K. ROACH

Houghton Mifflin Company Boston 1980

Library of Congress Cataloging in Publication Data

Roach, Marilynne K
  Down to earth at Walden.

  SUMMARY: Describes the practical aspects of
Thoreau's day-to-day life at Walden and the 19th-
century world surrounding him.
  1. Thoreau, Henry David, 1817-1862 – Homes and
haunts – Massachusetts – Walden Pond region – Juvenile
literature. 2. Thoreau, Henry David, 1817-1862.
Walden – Juvenile literature. 3. Walden Pond region,
Mass. – Biography – Juvenile literature. 4. Authors,
American – 19th century – Biography – Juvenile literature.
[1. Thoreau, Henry David, 1817-1862. 2. Authors,
American. 3. United States – Social life and customs –
1783-1865] I. Title.
PS3053.R58 818'309 [B] [92] 80-15248
ISBN 0-395-29647-1

P 10 9 8 7 6 5 4 3 2 1

CONTENTS

Introduction   vii

Biography I   1

Walden Pond — Former Scenes   5

Geology   10

Fitchburg Railroad   13

Irish Shanties   15

Building   18

Furnishings   32

Food   35

Clothing   39

Fuel   41

Money and Jobs   46

The Bean-Field   49

Woodchucks (Marmota Monax)   55

Surveying   60

Ice Cutting   63

Indians   69

Former Inhabitants and Visitors   72

Nature   79

Biography II   82

Afterword   85

Bibliography   87

c. 1

Introduction

THE CORE OF *Walden* is its philosophy, presented in a framework of Thoreau's daily life during his sojourn at Walden Pond. This book attempts to enlarge only on the material parts of *Walden*, the day-to-day living and the how-to, for Thoreau the philosopher was also a practical man.

Biography I

⚘⚘⚘

Henry David Thoreau (pronounced *Thorr*-oh) was born in Concord, Massachusetts, July 12, 1817, in his grandmother's farmhouse on the Virginia Road, and baptized David Henry Thoreau. Because the family always called him Henry, he later reversed the names. Except for a few years, Thoreau lived all his life in Concord, "the most estimable place in all the world," although he moved frequently within the town itself.

His father, John Thoreau (1787–1859), experienced various financial troubles (among them a crooked partner) in his efforts at storekeeping, so that times were lean until he hit on making pencils. His mother, Cynthia Dunbar (1787–1872), helped make ends meet by taking in boarders; there were always people coming and going among the family, including an assortment of aunts and an uncle.

Henry was the third of four children: Helen (1812–1849), the quiet elder sister who died of tuberculosis; John, Jr. (1815–1842), the more outgoing of the brothers; Henry (1817–1862); and Sophia (1819–1876), who helped edit Henry's last essays and, after his death, ran the family graphite business. All the Thoreau children taught school at one time or another, and all learned appreciation of nature from their parents. None of the four married.

For a few years the family lived in Boston, on the poor side of Beacon Hill, while John, Sr., taught school. The summer of Henry's fifth birthday they drove out from Boston to Concord to visit Cynthia's mother and picnic at Walden Pond. "It is one of the oldest scenes stamped on my memory," he wrote about a quarter century later.

At the age of sixteen Thoreau entered Harvard (the family having managed to scrape together the $179 yearly combined expenses, helped by a partial scholarship), where he did well despite absences caused by the beginning of tuberculosis.

When he graduated in 1837, he had already become acquainted with his fellow townsman Ralph Waldo Emerson, the principal American transcendental philosopher of his day. It was fortunate for Thoreau that several literary and philosophical minds gravitated to Concord at various times (Bronson Alcott, Ellery Channing, Margaret Fuller, Nathaniel Hawthorne), for even with a love for solitude it is difficult for writers and thinkers to create in a vacuum. His first published piece appeared in the local newspaper in 1837—an anonymous obituary.

In the same year Thoreau began teaching in Concord's Center School. But when a member of the school board insisted he flog the students for discipline, Thoreau chose six

2

at random, smacked them with a switch, and quit. Unfortunately, neither the class nor the officials got the point he intended to dramatize.

The country was in a depression and jobs were hard to come by. He worked in his father's pencil shop and, although he improved the formulas and machines they used, it wasn't the line of work he wanted. Eventually he started a private school—his brother John soon joined him in the venture—which offered such innovations as field trips and nature walks. Boys and girls from distant places (two were from Cuba) could board at the Thoreaus' house. It succeeded well for three years, only to be disbanded when John fell ill of tuberculosis. Before this, the brothers had taken a rowboat trip up the Concord and Merrimack rivers to the White Mountains, and fallen in love with Ellen Sewell, who refused them both.

When the school closed, Emerson invited Thoreau to stay with his family as live-in handyman and gardener. In January 1842, John, Jr., contracted lockjaw from a small cut and died suddenly and painfully. Henry, who had been tending him, experienced a psychosomatic version of the same disease, so intense was his grief. (It was a terrible month: Emerson's young son died of scarlet fever at the same time.)

3

The following year Thoreau accepted a tutoring position with the family of William Emerson (RWE's brother) on Staten Island in New York. Although he made some contact with the Manhattan publishing world, he was so profoundly homesick that he moved back to Concord—permanently—before the year was out.

He seemed to be convinced that Concord was the place for him to be, and writing the thing to do even if he couldn't make a living at it. As there were no wife and children dependent on him, he could in good conscience earn just enough to live on by day labor and still have enough time for observing nature and writing.

Many of his townsfolk could not appreciate such a decision and assumed he was just lazy. It didn't help when, in the spring of 1844, Thoreau and a neighbor, Edward Hoar, accidently burned the woods near Fair Haven Bay when their campfire flared out of control.

On the brighter side, his inventions had improved the family pencil business enough so they could have a house of their own for the first time. Mrs. Thoreau selected a lot on Texas Street, across the railroad tracks at the edge of the village, and Henry and his father built it, Henry digging and stoning the cellar foundations.

About the same time, Emerson bought a wood-lot at Walden and, in the spring of 1845, Thoreau arranged to build a small house there.

Walden Pond –
Former Scenes

♣♣♣

In Thoreau's day the land about Walden was not deep, impenetrable forest, but rather semi-open, shrubby wood-lots. Some hills, like Haywood's Peak, were bare, and it was possible to stand on the bedrock of Emerson's Cliff and see across the new growth as far as the Peterborough range in New Hampshire on a clear day.

Some sixty years earlier the thick forest had sheltered moose, bear, deer, and eagles—all gone by Thoreau's time—and trees crowded to the shore of the pond, whose surface was alive with migrating ducks in their seasons. The Walden Road, heading to Wayland in one direction, was built on logs over a maple swamp (later turned to farmland) as it headed northward toward Concord Village. Various people lived along it from time to time: a family of freed slaves, a solitary workman, the town drunkard.

5

Wyman the potter claimed an iron chest sometimes floated to Walden's surface, but if anyone approached, it would sink again. More certainly there were sunken tree trunks like huge jackstraws, and a clumsy old dug-out canoe that no one owned but which all the fishermen used. By Thoreau's boyhood the canoe and most of the drowned trees had rotted away, but the trees still overhung much of the shore, festooned in places with curtains of grapevines.

Thoreau had considered living off by himself for several years. During a vacation from Harvard he and a school friend, Charles Stearns Wheeler, camped in a cabin by Flint's Pond. He almost bought the Hollowell Farm a few years before the Walden experiment, but the deal fell through, rather to his relief: he didn't want a farm—it was the weeds and wild things on it that attracted him.

Since his purpose was not to set up a permanent household but to live an experiment in economy and find enough uninterrupted time for a long stint of writing and thinking, Thoreau considered such sites as Flint's Pond (the owner flatly refused), Fair Haven Hill, Baker Farm, and others, as well as his beloved Walden.

While out for a walk in the fall of 1844, Emerson chanced to meet some men interested in selling an eleven-acre briar patch near Walden Pond. With little hesitation he bought it for $8.10 an acre and, a few days later, bought an adjacent pine grove for $125 more. Although he toyed with the idea of building a study there for himself, he gave Thoreau permission to build on the site in return for clearing some of the scrub and replanting it with pines. (In 1845 Emerson purchased forty more acres across the pond—Emerson's Cliff.)

Emerson even signed over the lot to Thoreau in his will—just in case—but everyone's health held up and Thoreau signed it back when the experiment was over.

Thus, in the spring of 1845, Thoreau chose the site for his one-room house on the slope above his favorite cove, "about a mile and a half south of the village of Concord and somewhat higher than it," a mile from any neighbor, where he had "a distant view of the railroad where it touches the pond on the one hand, and of the fence which skirts the woodland road on the other."

It was about a half-hour walk up the tracks to his family's home, yet the spot could seem as remote as the Western prairies—which he had also considered, but rejected.

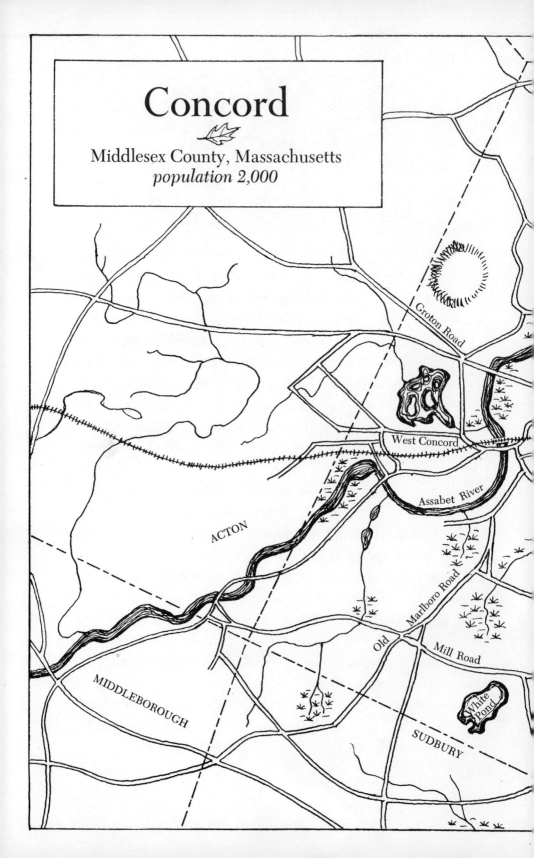

Concord

Middlesex County, Massachusetts
population 2,000

Groton Road

West Concord

Assabet River

ACTON

Old Marlboro Road

Mill Road

MIDDLEBOROUGH

White Pond

SUDBURY

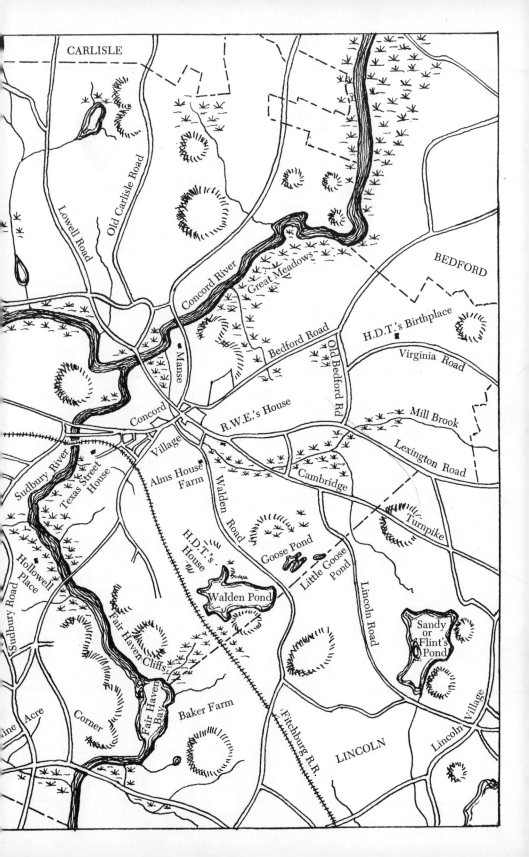

Geology

The Ice Age, which shaped so much of New England's land-scape, was only the latest of at least eleven in earth's history. It began about a million years ago with a gradual increase of cool days each year until summer disappeared from much of the Northern Hemisphere. Thousands of years of blizzards pressed down on the heart of Labrador. The snow compressed to ice until the accumulation reached about two hundred feet, and the mass began to spread outward from its own weight—a glacier.

It spread over southern Canada, was joined by other glaciers to form the Laurentide Ice Cap, dug out the Great

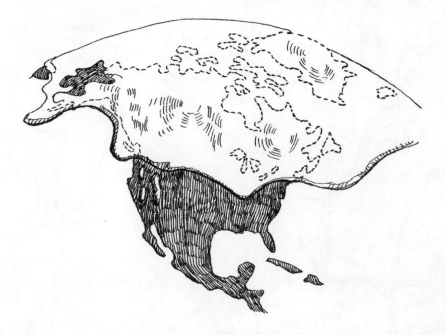

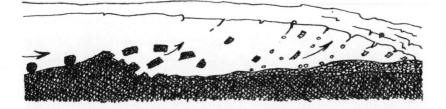

Lakes, and engulfed all of New England. It enclosed even the highest mountains, ground down the northern sides of rocky hills and plucked stones from their southern faces, scraped grooves into the bedrock, and peeled off all soil.

About 12,000 years ago it began to melt by stages. Long Island and Cape Cod were formed from debris left by the receding edge, while dirt, pebbles, and boulders settled to the earth far from their sources. Ice-walled lakes formed over Concord and Boston. Detached chunks of ice, embedded and insulated in silt, lasted long after the glacier itself had retreated. When these did melt, their spaces became pond-holes in the new layers of soil. As many, especially on Cape Cod where they were first studied, are round, these are called kettle-hole ponds. But plenty of them are irregular, like Walden.

Thoreau tells of the legend, then current in Concord, that once there had been a hill in place of Walden, but a tribe of Indians gathered there, offended the gods, so the hill shook and collapsed, killing all save one old woman named Walden. Except that Walden is an English place name, the legend has an odd similarity to fact. Parts of Alaskan glaciers covered with enough dirt to support modest groves of trees, just like regular hills, have been observed in the twentieth century. It is estimated that the first humans in the region, the Paleo-Indians, arrived some 10,500 years ago.

So there appeared Walden, with no visible stream leading in or out, rising and falling over the years by several feet—enough to flood and drain temporary coves, or reveal sand bars—but in a rhythm unlike that of the other ponds of the region. Many thought it was bottomless or connected to vast subterranean rivers.

Instead, as geologist Eugene H. Walker discovered, the lack of surface streams, plus the texture of the sand and gravel hills, delays the noticeable effects of rainfall or drought. The level of the pond is the level of the water table. The watershed absorbs rain before it can form into brooks, while the outflow partly seeps into a nearby swamp, the rest absorbed through the roots of surrounding vegetation, or exhaled into the air.

Fitchburg Railroad

⚘⚘⚘

The Fitchburg Railroad reached Concord in 1844, gashing the western shore of Walden as it passed. Before this time the only regular public transportation through Concord was the mail coaches between Boston and Leominster, Massachusetts, or Keene, New Hampshire. Teamsters hauled goods and a few riders in their wagons, while drovers herded cattle down the roads to the market towns.

Once the trains came—six a day in each direction, speeding along at twenty miles an hour—nearly everything was shipped in box cars, and the teamsters rioted. But there was little call for them anymore, or for the drovers, or for the inns that had dotted their long routes. Factories operating upstream on water power, as in West Concord, had easy access to the great port cities. Farmers, instead of growing mostly staples for themselves that could last the winter, began to specialize in perishable fruits and vegetables they could now ship quickly to Boston markets.

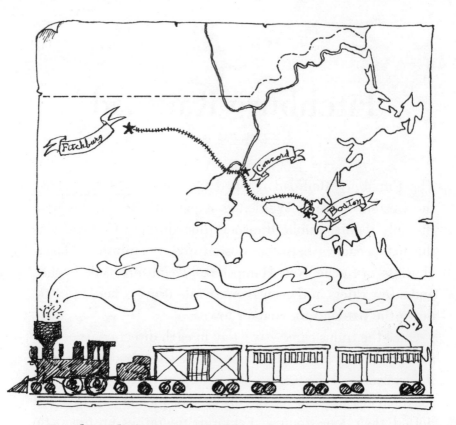

People no longer estimated time by sun and season alone. The trains "go and come with such regularity and precision, and their whistle can be heard so far, that the farmers set their clocks by them, and thus one well conducted institution regulates a whole country."

Authors like Emerson, and later Thoreau, were able to travel to lecture before the many lyceums sprouting in the region. Emerson also owned a few shares of stock in the railroad, and had sold some woodland for the track's right-of-way (but no more than the minimum). Locomotives weren't without drawbacks. Chestnut trees became railroad ties, while oak and maple fueled the engines. Furthermore, sparks from the smokestacks set frequent fires in adjacent wood-lots.

Irish Shanties

The Irish laborers who built the railroad, and their families, were temporarily housed in shanty towns along the track. (The Irish "seantig," pronounced "shanty," means hut.) As the work moved on, some families stayed, the men getting work as farm hands, the women as household help. This was the first large group with a different background, religion, and often, language, to settle in the country towns of the region since their founding. Inevitably there was friction, although the Irish were soon enough out of the shanties and into better quarters.

One of the shanty towns was near the Deep Cut not far from Walden; Nathaniel Hawthorne saw it in 1843. The huts crouched among the trees strung with washing lines. Hawthorne thought the earth piled outside their walls for insulation made the houses look as natural there as mushrooms.

Thoreau and his father built the pencil shop ell to the Texas Street house with recycled shanty boards sold off from vacated huts. As part of the materials for his Walden house, Thoreau bought James Collins's "uncommonly fine" shanty for $4.25.

"It was of small dimensions, with a peaked cottage roof, and not much else to be seen, the dirt being raised five feet all around as if it were a compost heap." The roof was warped and the family's hens went in and out under the door. Inside, the floor was dirt except for a few boards set down, and there was a window—an unusual feature—"of two whole squares originally, only the cat had passed out that way lately. There was a stove, a bed, and a place to sit, an infant in the house where it was born, a silk parasol, gilt-framed looking-glass, and a patent new coffee mill nailed to an oak sapling, all told."

Other families had less than the Collinses; Thoreau knew of one household that possessed two each of plates, bowls, and spoons, plus a knife with no handle, whose bed was coarse sheets over a little straw on a board. They saved every penny to bring the rest of their children to America.

In Ireland thousands lived with their animals in one-room mud huts four or five feet high, roofed with boughs or turf. The fire burned in the center of the dirt floor under a smoke-hole in the roof. (Landlords could evict tenants at any time.)

They depended exclusively on potatoes because it was the only crop they could grow in sufficient quantity on the tiny plots they could afford to rent. A blight rotted the potatoes in Ireland (as well as in Europe and elsewhere) in 1846, when Thoreau lived at Walden, starting the great potato famine.

Building

"The necessaries of life for man in this climate," Thoreau estimated, are "Food, Shelter, Clothing, and Fuel; for not till we have secured these are we prepared to entertain the true problems of life with freedom and a prospect of success."

Having selected a site above the northwestern cove near "a small open field in the woods where pine and hickories were springing up," Thoreau began with shelter. "Near the end of March, 1845, I borrowed an axe and went down to the woods by Walden Pond, nearest to where I intended to build my house, and began to cut down some tall arrowy white pines, still in their youth, for timber."

The axe belonged to Alcott, or possibly Emerson or Channing. At any rate, "I returned it sharper than I received it . . . So I went on for some days cutting and hewing timber, and also studs and rafters, all with my narrow axe . . . I hewed the main timbers six inches square, most of the studs on two sides only, and the rafters and floor timbers on one side, leaving the rest of the bark on, so that they were just as

straight and much stronger than sawed ones." (This was an old technique. Hawthorne's pre-Revolutionary "Old Manse" in Concord was built this way.) "Each stick was carefully mortised or tenoned by its stump, for I had borrowed other tools by then."

Materials purchased were as follows:

Boards,	$ 8.03½	*Mostly shanty boards.*
Refuse shingles for roof and sides,	4.00	
Laths,	1.25	
Two second-hand windows with glass,	2.34	
One thousand old brick,	4.00	
Two casks of lime,	2.40	*That was high.*
Hair,	0.31	*More than I needed.*
Mantle-tree iron,	0.15	
Nails,	3.90	
Hinges and screws,	0.14	
Latch,	0.10	
Chalk,	0.01	
Transportation,	1.40	*I carried a good part on my back.*
In all,	$28.12½	

The windows he thought overpriced, but the latch he helped to forge himself. The $4.25 worth of Collins's shanty boards included what nails he could salvage, but a bystander stole them.

19

"I dug my cellar in the side of a hill sloping to the south, where a woodchuck had formerly dug his burrow, down through sumach and blackberry roots, and the lowest stain of vegetation, six feet square by seven deep, to a fine sand where potatoes would not freeze in any winter. The sides were left shelving, and not stoned; but the sun having never shone on them, the sand still keeps its place. It was but two hours' work."

Thoreau says nothing about foundations. The site excavated by Roland Robbins a century later revealed stone piers about ten by twenty inches at each corner, and at the center of each long side. (Their locations, however, would have made the house larger than the ten by fifteen feet Thoreau mentioned.) The wooden sills would have rested on the piers.

The house was framed by mid-April, and one afternoon at the beginning of May several of his friends came by for the house-raising: the philosophers Ralph Waldo Emerson (unfortunately ten-thumbed) and Bronson Alcott (who had grown up on a farm and so was handy enough); the brothers George and Burrill Curtis (recently from the failed communal experiment of Brook Farm); Ellery Channing (one of the few who could keep up with Thoreau's walks but whose attempts to follow his poetic bent led him to neglect his family); and the practical Concord farmer Edmund Hosmer, with his sons John, Edmund, and Andrew.

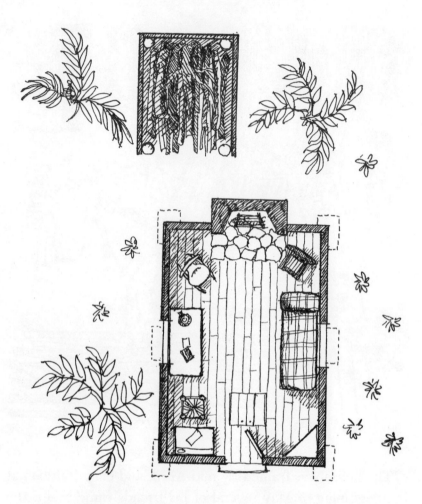

With the frame in place, Thoreau lugged two cartloads of stones up from the pond in his arms, and made a chimney foundation roughly five feet square. He bound it with mortar at key points and chinked it with bits of broken bricks, the technique he and his father had used in building the family's house the year before. Smooth hearthstones were later fitted over this rough foundation, but as it was summer he put off building the hearth, and he cooked outdoors behind the house.

Next he boarded and roofed the frame with planks from Collins's shanty, dried and straightened and "carefully feather-edged and lapped, so that it was perfectly impervious to rain." And of course he put down a rough first floor with a trap door to the cellar. There were enough leftovers to make a small open woodshed behind the house. On the subject of privies, he remained silent.

"Drive a nail home," Thoreau wrote, "and clinch it so faithfully that you can wake up in the night and think of your work with satisfaction." It has been estimated that the $3.90 worth of square-cut nails he bought was enough to build a regular-sized house. The cellar-hole excavated in 1945 contained hundreds of bent nails.

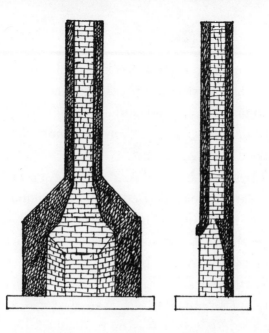

He moved in on July 4, 1845, but had to spend his time fighting the weeds in his bean-field. So for the first summer his house "was merely a defence against the rain, without plastering or chimney, the walls being of rough weather-stained boards, with wide chinks, which made it cool at night. The upright white hewn studs and freshly planed door and window casings gave it a clean and airy look, especially in the morning, when the timbers were saturated with dew."

When he got around to the chimney, he first had to clean old mortar from his "one thousand old brick" with a trowel. "The mortar on them was fifty years old, and was said to be still growing harder . . . I picked out as many fireplace bricks as I could find, to save work and waste, and I filled the spaces between the bricks about the fireplace with stones from the pond shore, and also made my mortar with the white sand from the same place."

He set only a few courses of bricks a day, somehow keeping them moist between times, for brick leaches the moisture from mortar, causing it to dry and separate instead of bond.

Channing stayed on a few weeks to help with all this winterizing. He had to sleep on the floor since, as he said, "Two was one too much in this house."

"My dwelling was small," Thoreau admitted, "and I could hardly entertain an echo in it."

"When I began to have a fire at evening, before I plastered my house, the chimney carried smoke particularly well, because of the numerous chinks between the boards. Yet I passed some cheerful evenings in that cool and airy apartment, surrounded by the rough brown boards full of knots, and rafters with the bark on high over-head. My house never pleased my eye so much after it was plastered, though I was obliged to confess that it was more comfortable."

Next he set about nailing four dollars' worth of "refuse shingles" on the roof and exterior walls. But they were "imperfect and sappy shingles made of the first slice of the log, whose edges I was obliged to straighten with a plane." He also put down a second, more finished floor.

"I did not plaster till it was freezing weather." It was mid-November and much too late in the season for such a task. It seems only luck that the plaster didn't freeze and crack off. "I brought over some whiter and cleaner sand for this purpose from the opposite shore of the pond in a boat . . . In lathing I was pleased to be able to send home each nail with a single blow of the hammer, and it was my ambition to transfer the plaster from the board to the wall neatly and rapidly."

He had experimented with extracting lime from the shells of fresh-water clams, but for his house he bought two casks of lime, mixed it with water, added the sand for strength, and horsehair to bind it.

"I admired anew the economy and convenience of plastering, which so effectively shuts out the cold and takes a handsome finish, and I learned the various casualties to which the plasterer is liable."

He finished up on Wednesday, November 12, dumped the excess plaster in front of the door to level the ground (he later covered it with soil), and spent the next two weeks in town while the plaster miraculously dried.

"I have thus a tight shingled and plastered house, ten feet wide by fifteen long, and eight-feet posts, with a garret and a closet, a large window on each side, two trap doors, one door at the end, and a brick fireplace opposite."

All for $28.12½.

Furnishings

🌲🌲🌲

When grumbling about convenience and independence, Thoreau wrote, "I would rather sit on a pumpkin and have it all to myself, than be crowded on a velvet cushion." However, it wasn't necessary to go to such extremes. "None is so poor that he need sit on a pumpkin. That is shiftlessness. There is a plenty of such chairs as I like best in the village garrets to be had for taking them away. Furniture! Thank God, I can sit and I can stand without the aid of a furniture warehouse."

What he did have he loaded into a hay-rig and took to Walden in one trip: a bed with a caned center he made himself, a three-legged table, and three chairs ("one for solitude, two for friendship, three for society"). The one for solitude was a plain Windsor chair to which Thoreau attached homemade rockers. Although the house had no lock, his green slant-topped desk did, for he was frugal with his paper supply and considered his manuscripts private.

For the fireplace he had a pair of tongs and andirons, plus a frying pan, a skillet, and a kettle for cooking, two knives and forks, three plates, one cup, one spoon, and a dipper. The washbowl and the mirror three inches in diameter must have been joined—though he didn't say so—by his shaving kit, as he was clean-shaven until 1856.

There was a jug for molasses in his closet, another jug for lamp oil, and a japanned lamp. The closet itself, perhaps a wall cabinet or a full-length corner cupboard, is a puzzle. The only thing known about it is that someone, probably Sophia, drew a picture on its door of Thoreau and the mouse that lived under the house.

His books and writing materials occupied desk and table, along with various scientific instruments he had at one time or another—for he did some surveying, took water temperatures with a Fahrenheit thermometer, and gazed at battling ants through a magnifying lens while they were confined under a glass tumbler.

Except for bedding and clothes, his flute, umbrella, and a broom, that was probably all. Outside he had a few tools— hoe, spade, and axe—his homemade wheelbarrow, and the rowboat he had built and wheeled over to Walden from the Concord River.

He used no curtains, for only the sun and moon looked in, and declined the offer of a mat because it required more care than it offered convenience. Similarly, he had three white stones on his desk, but tossed them out the window when he realized the time taken to dust them could better be used dusting a dusty mind. That, of course, was to indicate the principle of the thing. His garret room in the family home caused his sister Sophia to remark (he recorded), "that I regard the dust on my furniture like the bloom on fruits, not to be swept off."

Food

♈♈♈

"As I did not work hard," wrote Thoreau (disregarding his daily ten- and twenty-mile walks), "I did not have to eat hard, and it cost me but a trifle for my food."

Many meals in Thoreau's day were heavy affairs. He mentioned farm hands coming in from the fields for a noon meal of "boiled beef and cider and Indian bread." "I did not use tea, nor coffee, nor butter, nor milk, nor fresh meat, and so did not have to work to get them." That was his preference, but tea was included with supplies on the Maine Woods expedition, and if someone served him meat he ate it.

"I sometimes caught a mess of fish for my dinner, and once I went so far as to slaughter a woodchuck which ravaged my bean-field . . . and devour him."

He grew twelve bushels of beans the first year, but traded most of them for rice, which he preferred, plus some green corn and potatoes. In March of 1846 he figured his expenses for the previous eight months, from July 4:

Rice,	$1.73½	
Molasses,	1.73	*Cheapest form of the saccharine.*
Rye meal,	1.04¾	
Indian meal,	0.99¾	*Cheaper than rye.*
Pork,	0.22	
Flour,	0.88	*Costs more than Indian meal, both money and trouble.*
Sugar,	0.80	
Lard,	0.65	
Apples,	0.25	
Dried apples,	0.22	
Sweet potatoes,	0.10	
One pumpkin,	0.06	
One watermelon,	0.02	
Salt,	0.03	

All experiments which failed.

Yes, I did eat, $8.74. All told.

He estimated that his food cost twenty-seven cents a week.

He cooked outdoors the first summer in a stone-lined fire pit up behind the house. If it rained he set up boards. By fall he had built the indoor fireplace and, in the second year, installed a small stove.

The twenty-seven cents weekly provided bread of "rye and Indian meal without yeast, potatoes, rice, a very little salt pork, molasses, and salt; and my drink water. It was fit that I should live on rice, mainly, who loved so well the philosophy of India." To this he sometimes added, "ears of green sweet-corn boiled," or boiled and salted purslane, a weed from his cornfield, now known to be rich in vitamin C (originally brought to this country as a garden crop), "wild apples for coddling," several varieties of berries in season, wild grapes, and chestnuts—abundant then—which, he felt, "were a good substitute for bread" (as James Boswell had noticed in eighteenth-century Corsica).

Thoreau mentions "a thin dish of gruel," but more often a hasty-pudding (cornmeal, molasses, salt, and water). "However, only one or two of my guests were ever bold enough to stay and eat a hasty-pudding with me; but when they saw that crisis approaching they beat a hasty retreat rather." Some guests simply brought a picnic lunch made up at the grocery in town: fried turnovers, cheese, and cake.

He experimented with baking bread on a stick over the fire, but it got smoky and tasted of pine. Small loaves worked better, or dough spread thinly on hot rocks. He gave up using yeast, which he had to bring from town, after the bottle exploded in his pocket more than once.

He drank Walden water. "In the warmest weather I usually placed a pailful in my cellar, where it became cool in the night, and remained so during the day." In the hottest weather he went a half mile to Brister's Spring.

Occasionally he ate at the homes of friends, as had been his custom before coming to Walden. This was enough for some townsfolk to consider him a parasite.

One of his guests, Joseph Hosmer, survived Thoreau's cooking and left an appreciative account of the meal: horned pout roasted on hot stones, some in wet paper and some not, heated-over beans, corn, thin unleavened bread baked on a hot stone, plus salt for the fish.

It has been estimated that his diet was, despite neighborhood criticism, nutritionally adequate.

Clothing

✝✝✝

"Let him who has work to do recollect that the true object of clothing is, first, to retain the vital heat, and secondly, in this state of society, to cover nakedness."

Ready-made clothes were not yet common and it sometimes took a little argument to get the local seamstress, Miss Mary Minot, to make something practical enough to suit him. He preferred Vermont gray homespun trousers that could stand to be walked through brush and briar, or, better yet, a weave of browns and greens for camouflage when observing animals. A clay-colored corduroy wasn't bad either, although he noticed the Yankees wouldn't wear it because of its Irish associations, and the Irish scorned it as too old-country.

Despite his shirt-sleeve reputation, the two photographs and the pencil portrait of Thoreau show him wearing a suit and tie. "Anything but black clothes."

A purely practical (male) wardrobe could be purchased reasonably: "A thick coat can be bought for five dollars, which will last as many years, thick pantaloons for two dollars, cowhide boots for a dollar and a half a pair, a summer hat for a quarter of a dollar, and a winter cap for sixty-two and a half cents, or a better be made at home at a nominal cost."

Thoreau's original invention in this line was his "botany hat": an ordinary size-seven straw hat with its lining gathered halfway up the crown to form a shelf which held botanical specimens. Once he brought home a frog in it.

Fuel

✿✿✿

"Some spoke as if I were going to the woods in order to
freeze myself." Instead, his woodshed held two or three cords
of small pine and hickory stumps pulled from his bean-field.
"The dead and for the most part unmerchantable wood behind my house, and driftwood from the pond, have supplied
the remainder of my fuel."

"In this town the price of wood rises almost steadily, and
the only question is, how much higher it is to be this year
than it was the last." In 1846 wood cost four dollars a cord
in Middlesex County, and it was then estimated a family
would burn thirteen to fourteen cords a year.

41

The land about Walden was principally wood-lots, where owners culled a tree here and a tree there for their own use and so kept a constant supply growing. Or an owner would have the whole lot cut down at once—Haywood's Peak just south of Thoreau's house was bare when he mapped the pond —and sell it commercially, for wood was still the main fuel in America. Professional woodchoppers like Alek Therien were always about their business.

Thoreau had found an old axe head in the woods and made a hickory handle for it. With this he found, as he had been told, that wood kept him warm twice—once while chopping it and again when burning it. He scavenged dead wood, abandoned fences, and a raft of pine logs left behind by the railroad workers.

"A few pieces of fat pine were a great treasure . . . In previous years I had often gone 'prospecting' over some bare hill-side, where a pitch-pine wood had formerly stood, and got out the fat pine roots. They are almost indestructible."

Locating a rotten stump, he dug and chopped his way to the root, "yellow as beef tallow, or as if you had struck on a vein of gold, deep into the earth."

Ordinarily, however, he kindled his fire with dry leaves, which he stored in his shed, and sometimes "green hickory finely split" as the woodchoppers made their campfires. "Hard green wood just cut, though I used but little of that, answered my purpose better than any other."

As he often left a fire burning when he left the house, to come back to a warm room, it was fortunate there was only one accident. While splitting kindling he happened to look in the window just after a spark had landed on his bed. He extinguished it before it burned more than the span of his hand.

"The next winter I used a small cooking-stove for economy, since I did not own the forest . . . The stove not only took up room and scented the house, but it concealed the fire, and I felt as if I had lost a companion."

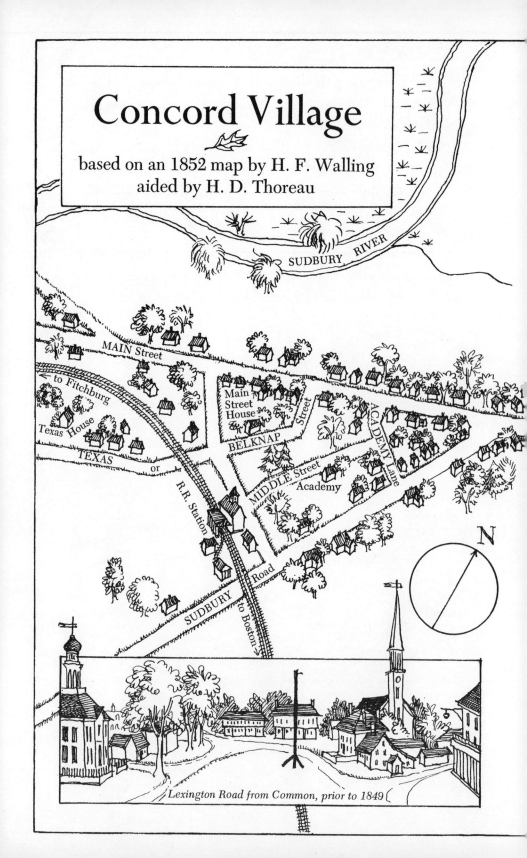

Concord Village

based on an 1852 map by H. F. Walling
aided by H. D. Thoreau

SUDBURY RIVER

MAIN Street

to Fitchburg

Texas House

TEXAS or

Main Street House

BELKNAP

Street

MIDDLE Street

Academy

ACADEMY Lane

R.R. Station

SUDBURY Road

to Boston

N

Lexington Road from Common, prior to 1849

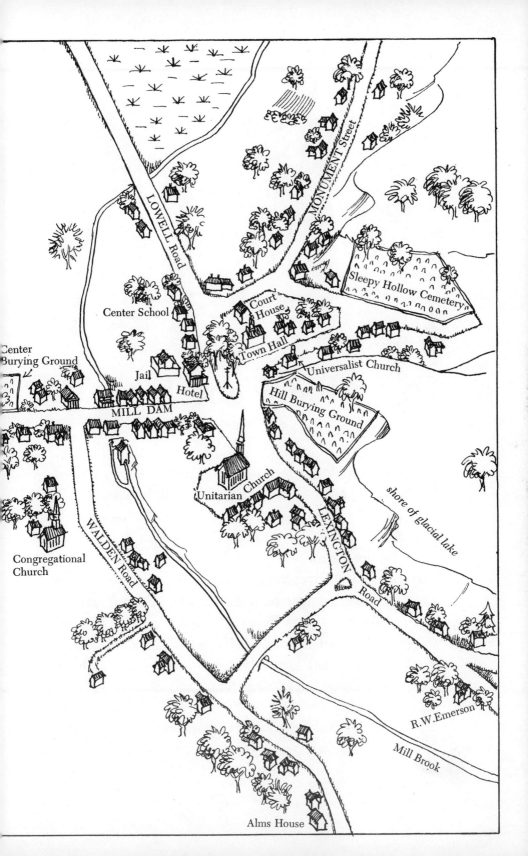

Money and Jobs

†††

Thoreau scrupulously itemized his Walden expenses to prove
his point that one can live adequately with little money. The
real "cost of a thing," he wrote, "is the amount of what I will
call life which is required to be exchanged for it, immediately
or in the long run."

In the mid-nineteenth century a dollar was the usual payment for a man's twelve-hour day of physical labor—six days a
week. (Women's work brought a half to a third of a man's
wages.) Thoreau remembered when laborers building the
Fitchburg Railroad got only sixty cents a day. The pro-
fessionals earned more, but Thoreau's day labor usually
earned a dollar.

"An average house in this neighborhood costs perhaps eight
hundred dollars, and to lay up this sum will take from ten to

fifteen years of the laborer's life, even if he is not encumbered with a family." The country rates for rent, he tells us, ran from twenty-five to a hundred dollars yearly.

"I found, that by working about six weeks a year, I could meet all the expenses of living. The whole of my winters, as well as most of my summers, I had free and clear for study." Observation and writing were his real, if usually unpaid, work.

Thoreau's seemingly casual attitude toward earning a living caused a good deal of gossip among the townsfolk. Nevertheless, he took great care to avoid debt, and never assumed responsibilities he didn't fulfill to the letter. As Emerson said, Thoreau would "pay every debt as if God wrote the bill." He paid room and board while living in his parents' house, which for some years his mother ran as a boarding house. He was just as careful to *be* paid by others for work done.

"I have as many trades as fingers," he wrote in *Walden*. And when the secretary of his class at Harvard sent him a questionnaire for the tenth reunion (which he did not attend), he answered: "I am a Schoolmaster—a private Tutor, a Surveyor—a Gardener, a Farmer—a Painter, I mean a House Painter, a Carpenter, a Mason, a Day-Laborer, a Pencil-Maker, a Glass-paper [sandpaper] Maker, a Writer, and sometimes a Poetaster." He would also shovel manure if necessary (75 cents), but preferred lecturing. Many of his essays and book chapters began as lectures, but audiences did not always get the point of his philosophy. However, the Salem Lyceum paid him twenty dollars for one lecture.

He also worked occasionally in his father's pencil factory —a small workshop in an ell of the house—and with his father discovered a formula to produce an evenly textured graphite paste that made their drawing pencils as fine as any imported from Europe. Thoreau invented a machine to saw the raw graphite, and another to grind it to the required fineness. The pencils sold for twenty-five cents each (when lesser brands cost fifty cents a dozen) and won J. Thoreau & Co. several prizes at trade fairs.

Eventually surveying became his principal means of making a living.

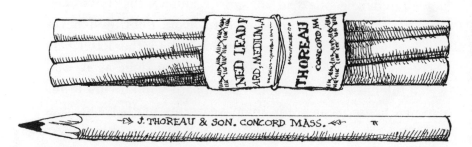

The Bean-Field

🌲🌲🌲

"Before I finished my house, wishing to earn ten or twelve dollars by some honest and agreeable method, in order to meet my unusual expenses, I planted about two acres and a half of light and sandy soil near it chiefly with beans, but also a small part with potatoes, corn, peas, and turnips."

The land had been cleared some fifteen years earlier and, according to one observer, had been heavily cropped with rye. More recently it had not been planted at all, but grown up to cinquefoil, blackberries, and johnswort, as well as pines and hickories. In the spring of 1845, Thoreau heaved out two or three cords of stumps, suitable for firewood, and planted his garden. "I was obliged to hire a team and a man for the ploughing, though I held the plough myself." He also moved a ground-bird's nest from harm's way, but the parent birds deserted it.

The bean rows were fifteen rods long (247½ feet), set "three feet by eighteen inches apart," stretching a total of seven miles between a blackberry patch and "a shrub oak copse where I could rest in the shade." The yellow upland soil was not the choicest. "One farmer said that it was 'good for nothing but to raise cheeping squirrels on.'"

Yet the beans grew fast enough so that the first were well sprouted before he planted the last rows. What with building the house, he had delayed planting until others were already busy hoeing. Passers-by seldom kept their opinions to themselves. They called out suggestions, recommending "a little chip dirt [dried dung], or any little waste stuff, or it may be ashes [potash] or plaster [lime or gypsum]." But he ignored their advice, as well as warnings not to hoe before the dew had dried, which he considered an old-wives' tale. (Actually, scattering the dew can spread mildew and rot.)

"Farmers far and near call it the paradise of beans," Thoreau noted in his *Journal*.

"When they were growing, I used to hoe from five o'clock in the morning till noon, and commonly spent the rest of the day about other affairs." But he often worked all day if necessary. "Removing the weeds, putting fresh soil about the bean stems, and encouraging this weed which I had sown, making the yellow soil express its summer thought in bean leaves and blossoms rather than in wormwood and piper and millet grass, making the earth say beans instead of grass."

Earth said beans best on the circles of mould where the rotting stumps had been. "My auxiliaries are the dews and rains which water this dry soil . . . My enemies are worms, cool days, and most of all woodchucks. The last have nibbled for me a quarter of an acre clean." If it weren't for the owls hunting rabbits in the field at night, the farmers concluded, Thoreau wouldn't have harvested anything. He admitted his garden was "the connecting link between wild and cultivated fields."

about ½ Acre shown

the Weeds

Purslane

Cinquefoil

St. John's wort

Blackberry

Roman Wormwood (Ragweed)

Sorrel

Piper

Millet

Pigweed

Nighthawk

Hen (Red-tailed) Hawk

(Passenger) Pigeon (extinct)

Brown Thrasher

Drop it, drop it, — cover it up, cover it up, — pull it up, pull it up, pull it up.

Salamander

However, he harvested "twelve bushels of beans, and eighteen bushels of potatoes, beside some peas and sweet corn. The yellow corn and turnips were too late to come to any thing."

In all, his expenses were:

For a hoe,	$ 0.54	
Ploughing, harrowing, and furrowing,	7.50	*Too much.*
Beans for seed,	3.12½	
Potatoes " "	1.33	
Peas " "	0.40	
Turnip seed,	0.06	
White line for crow fence,	0.02	
Horse cultivator and boy three hours,	1.00	
Horse and cart to get crop,	0.75	
In all,	$14.72½	

His income was:

Nine bushels and twelve quarts of beans sold,	$16.94
Five " large potatoes,	2.50
Nine " small,	2.25
Grass,	1.00
Stalks,	0.75
In all,	$23.44

(Grass and stalks go for cattle feed.) Therefore his profit was $8.71½, plus "produce consumed and on hand" worth $4.50.

For his own part, he considered the experiment successful, but planted only a third of an acre for his own use the following summer.

Woodchucks
(Marmota Monax)

The cellar of Thoreau's house occupied a woodchuck's abandoned den. But if that one had gone, there were still plenty in the neighborhood. Although there were acres and acres of unfarmed land, they preferred Thoreau's garden. "Look out for woodchucks," he warned, "if it is an exposed place, for they will nibble off the earliest tender leaves almost clean as they go; and again, when the young tendrils make their appearance, they have notice of it, and will shear them off with both buds and young pods, sitting erect like a squirrel."

Unlike most farmers of his time (or after), Thoreau realized that woodchucks had as much right to the world as he had. Nevertheless, his garden began to disappear before it could grow. According to one account—for he wrote little about this battle himself—he asked the local trappers how to catch the animal without using traps, and received only scorn. Thoreau had gotten rid of his gun long before, so he borrowed a trap and caught the woodchuck. He kept it captive for some hours, lectured it severely (or so it was reported in the village), then set it free, hoping for a truce.

A few days later it was back. Next the trap caught a skunk, which caused other problems. Eventually he trapped the chuck and carried it in his arms two miles away and let it go. However, another woodchuck appropriated the bean-field, and this one Thoreau killed and ate. It didn't taste too bad —rather musky—but he didn't consider the experiment worth repeating.

The cultivated beans must have been irresistibly succulent to the woodchucks compared to the available wild plants. They eat a wide variety of vegetable matter, including sorrel, dandelion, buttercups, plantain, daisy, hawkweed, clovers, and, in a pinch, sumach, goldenrod, Queen Anne's lace, and thistles. Part of the problem is that they must eat for two seasons at once to accumulate the layers of fat they live on throughout hibernation and early spring—for they wake before the plants begin to grow, and some starve to death in their burrows.

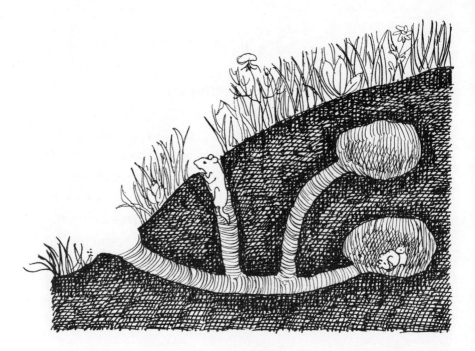

Adult woodchucks are about two feet long, weigh—at most —ten pounds, and can digest a third of their weight in vegetables a day, getting what moisture they need from the plants they eat. Although their brains are not very large, woodchucks are wily, curious, and capable of learning from experience. They grumble and chatter when surprised, and whistle for a signal. They are expert diggers who can climb trees if necessary.

Some years later, in April 1852, Thoreau cornered a woodchuck away from its burrow and knelt to examine it. The chuck chattered its teeth but they stared at each other for a half-hour until each felt sleepy. At last Thoreau was able to pat the animal. "I think I might learn some wisdom of him. His ancestors have lived here longer than mine. He is more thoroughly acclimated and naturalized than I."

Surveying

♈♈♈

When the Thoreau brothers taught school they preferred to demonstrate the value of their lessons by practical application. In 1840 Henry Thoreau bought a few basic instruments and took his mathematics class on field trips to practice surveying various Concord landforms, such as Fair Haven Cliffs.

Walden Pond was said to be bottomless, and some had claimed to have seen the great hole in its bottom that led all the way to the other side of the world, or perhaps only to some vast underground river flowing from the White Mountains. Thoreau classed these tales with Wyman's view of the spectral treasure chest, and set out to survey it "before the ice broke up, early in '46, with compass and chain and sounding line."

Others had attempted the task with a fifty-six-pound weight "and a wagon load of inch rope" to no avail. But Thoreau methodically cut holes in the ice and "fathomed it

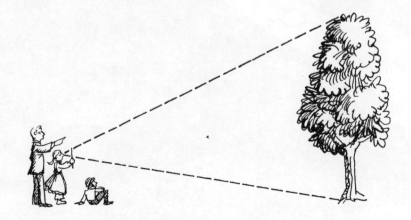

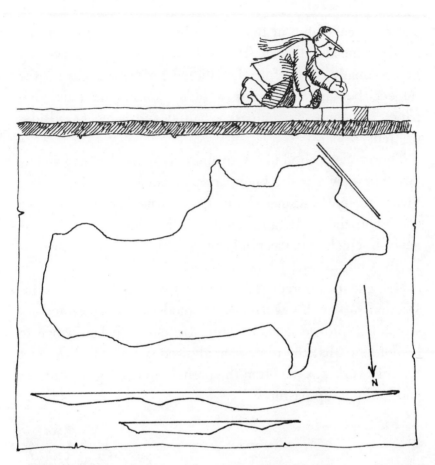

easily with a cod-line and a stone weighing about a pound
and a half."

He "mapped the pond by the scale of ten rods [165 feet]
to an inch, and put down the soundings, more than a hundred
in all," and drew careful profiles of the bottom's landscape.
(For his book he redrew it at forty rods [660 feet] to the
inch.) Walden, although relatively deep, was not the bottomless pit it was assumed to be. Modern scientists, in the late
1920s and early 1970s, armed with every new instrument,
only served to prove Thoreau correct in all his findings.

A few years later, in 1848, when he and his family suffered more financial setbacks, Thoreau decided to try surveying professionally. Therefore, he studied fourteen books on the subject, bought a surveyor, a blank journal, and drawing paper, and had his compass repaired and some broadsides printed.

Thoreau was hired to survey not only house lots and wood-lots, but new streets, boundaries of cemeteries and whole towns, the entire Concord River, and a field for a ploughing contest at the local fairground. He became Concord's surveyor-in-chief, and accepted assignments from as far away as Perth Amboy, New Jersey.

His clients appreciated his exactness and, as with his Walden survey, his work has, by modern standards and instruments, proved accurate still. He enjoyed the chance to be outdoors that the profession allowed, yet disliked the fact that his work was too often the prelude to cutting down trees and building up pastures.

Ice Cutting

As winter provided the only refrigeration, people cut ice and stored it, insulated by straw, in icehouses. Thoreau noticed that although Walden water often appeared green, it looked blue when frozen, "like solidified azure." Ice from the river was white, and that from the other ponds greenish.

Frederic Tudor, the "Ice King," who shipped ice all over the world, waged a trade war with his former partner, Nathaniel Jarvis Wyeth, who managed to get a monopoly of sources. Rather than buy from Wyeth, Tudor acquired cutting rights to Walden Pond during the winter of 1846–1847. For sixteen days Thoreau watched as a crew of "a hundred Irishmen, with Yankee overseers, came from Cambridge every day," by railroad with their equipment and a number of horses, "to get out the ice. They divided it into cakes by methods too well known to require description."

The well-known methods began with clearing snow from the surface by various horse-drawn scrapers. Then, guided by a tightly stretched rope, a horse-drawn ice plough scored a line some ten or a dozen rods (165–198 feet) along the ice.

Aided by various gauges the men further grooved the ice into twenty-two-inch squares. Then men with whipsaws cut it through in long strips. (They joked and invited Thoreau to work the underwater end as if they were cutting logs in a saw pit.)

The strips were poled along canals in the ice to the shallows, where another man with a spade-shaped chisel cut them into cakes twenty-two by forty-four inches. As these were scored in the middle, they could be broken into manageable squares when loaded on shipboard. (Less than twenty-five percent of the ice lasted long enough to reach its destination.)

Men hauled the cakes up an iron frame, its lower end supported on wood under water, its upper against the sled being loaded. Each sled held fourteen or fifteen cakes—about two tons—all pulled by one horse over the ice to the shore. There, near the railroad track, some sixty men with grappling irons stacked the ice in a pile some six or seven rods square (99–115½ feet), reaching thirty-five feet high on one side. More horses, hitched to block-and-tackle contrivances, raised the ice to the top. ("The horses invariably ate their oats out of cakes of ice hollowed out like buckets.")

They harvested about an acre a day—a thousand tons. The stack contained about ten thousand tons, insulated with hay and boarded over against wind erosion.

As it turned out, the Ice King won his trade war and went back to his usual sources of Fresh Pond and Spy Pond in Cambridge. The ice stacked at Walden remained until the following July, when it was unroofed and part taken away. The rest was left to melt under the sun, yet "it stood over that summer and the next winter, and was not quite melted till September 1848. Thus the pond recovered the greater part."

Indians

✝✝✝

Thoreau had a knack of finding Indian arrowheads. When a friend asked where to look for them, Thoreau reached down and picked one off the ground right by their feet. In Maine he surprised his Indian guide by finding some about the man's own village, although no one there had made any for generations.

Besides being sharp-eyed, Thoreau could estimate what sites would be most suitable for fishing or camping and thereby the most likely to have been lived in. He went out in the spring when thawing frost and melt-water erosion uncovered whole caches of stone tools, bowls, and weapons. While working in his bean-field, he found Indian implements, including a hearth—the circle of stones still fire-blackened. The very path about Walden was an Indian trail.

The cultures of New England had changed several times before the European migrations of the seventeenth century. The first people, called Paleo-Indians, arrived at the end of the last Ice Age, about 10,500 years ago, presumably as summer hunters on the tundra at the edge of the receding glacier. They flaked fluted spear points of flint brought from New York and hunted caribou and mammoth.

As the area warmed and became more forested, these people moved north after the herds, and were replaced by the Early Archaic people who lived from 7000 to 5000 years ago. Their spear points fit a socketed shaft and the hunters cast them with a wooden spear-thrower counterweighted with a carved stone—an atl-atl—to give a more powerful thrust. The Late Archaic people lived from 5000 years ago to A.D. 300 in a warmer, drier hardwood forest, in bark-covered houses that turned in on themselves like snail shells. They carved soapstone bowls for cooking; it has been speculated that before this invention food could only be roasted. However, it is possible to boil meals in leather bags or birch-bark boxes, as long as the liquid doesn't completely evaporate.

About A.D. 300 the Adena came from the Ohio Valley. Their culture had associations with the Mound-Builders of that region who, in turn, had similarities to the Aztecs of Mexico. The men used a new invention—a bow and arrows— to bring down game, and the women made ceramic vessels to cook in. Greatest of all, they possessed the knowledge of raising corn—maize.

The resulting hunting and farming culture, the Algonquin, lasted until the European settlers came, when there was a great plague of smallpox and other Old World diseases, to which the natives were not immune, and the greater part of the population died.

The Concord settlers were allotted their land by English authority, but made a point to settle, after a fashion, with the remaining Indians as well. In 1636 Reverend Peter Bulkley, Simon Willard, and others met under an oak in what became Concord Center with the local sachems, including Tahat-tawan, and the Squaw Sachem (the "Woman Chief"). The English made payment of wampum, hoes, hatchets, cotton cloth and shirts, plus, as a good-will gesture, a suit of English clothes to Webcowet, the Squaw Sachem's husband.

Former Inhabitants
and Visitors

❦❦❦

"Within the memory of many of my townsmen," wrote
Thoreau, "the road near which my house stands resounded
with the laugh and gossip of inhabitants, and the woods which
border it were notched and dotted here and there with their
little gardens and dwellings, though it was then much more
shut in by the forest than now."

The cellar-holes were still there, full of sumach and goldenrod, the clearings grown up with pines around the still-
blooming dooryard lilacs. Some of the inhabitants were
former slaves who were freed in Massachusetts by the Bill of
Rights in 1780, and given permission to build on their former
owners' lots. Besides day labor and gardening, they "pulled
wool," spun and wove linen and wool, parched corn, and
made pottery, baskets, stable brooms, and mats.

"East of my bean-field, across the road, lived Cato Ingraham, slave of Duncan Ingraham." Cato raised a grove of walnut trees by his small house on the path to Goose Pond—the wood was valued for fine furniture—"but a younger and whiter speculator got them at last." Presumably this is the same Cato who had a running fight alone in the woods with a rabid dog until he was able to kill it with an axe.

Zilpha White, former slave to a Mr. Spencer, had lived at the corner of Thoreau's bean-field with her cat, dog, and hens. During the War of 1812, some captured British soldiers in custody at Concord burned her tiny hovel with the animals locked inside. But she was out at the time; she lived on to the age of seventy-two, weaving flax and wool. As she was nearly blind by then, the Concord Female Charitable Society saw that she received a few necessities from time to time, including tea, tobacco, and brandy.

"Down the road, on the right hand, on Brister's Hill, lived Brister Freeman, 'a handy Negro,' slave of Squire Cummings once,—there where grow still the apple-trees which Brister planted and tended." His former owner willed him thirty-five pounds sterling, but had the selectmen administer it. Sometimes his name was written "Bristo." His gravestone reads "Scippio Brister." Both the hill and the spring are called "Brister's." He lived there with his wife, Fenda, who told fortunes, and their three children, but he outlived them all and died November 1, 1820, at the age of sixty-one.

Wyman the potter, who saw the magical chest rise in the pond, had his tiny shop among the hemlocks where the road passed closest to Walden's eastern end. His son also was a potter there for a time, but business was so poor that when the sheriff came to collect back taxes there was nothing at all to take but a chip of wood for form's sake.

Wyman's hut was later occupied by the Irishman Hugh Quoil (or Coyle or Cahill) and his wife. He was called Colonel Quoil because he had fought at the Battle of Waterloo, but he made his living in Concord by ditching. "He was a man of manners, like one who had seen the world, and was capable of more civil speech than you could well attend to." But shortly after Thoreau moved in, Quoil died in the road at the foot of Brister's Hill in "a fit of delirium-tremens," his obituary said, on October 1, 1845.

Did Quoil have his own still? "On Sundays, brother Irishmen and others, who had gone far astray from steady habits and the village, crossed my bean-field with empty jugs toward Quoil's . . . They went by sober, stealthy, silent . . . , returned loquacious, sociable, having long intended to call on you."

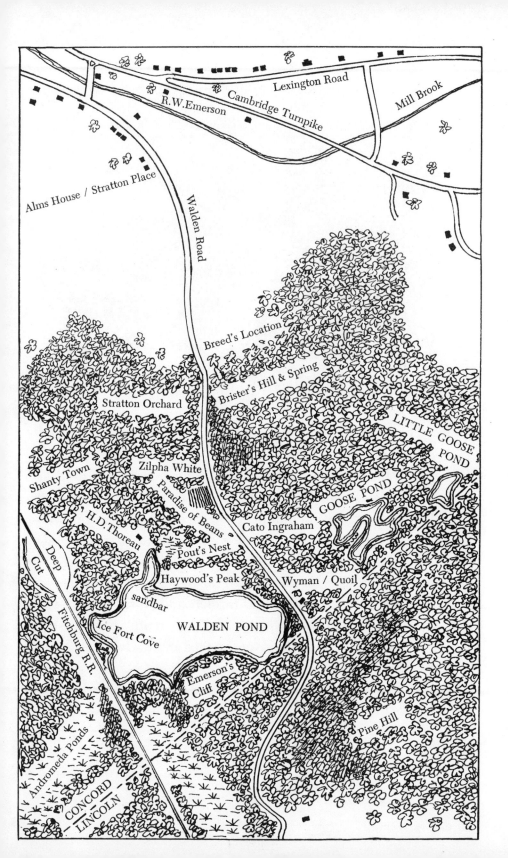

Lexington Road

R.W. Emerson

Cambridge Turnpike

Mill Brook

Alms House / Stratton Place

Walden Road

Breed's Location

Brister's Hill & Spring

Stratton Orchard

LITTLE GOOSE POND

Zilpha White

Shanty Town

Paradise of Beans

GOOSE POND

H.D. Thoreau

Cato Ingraham

Pout's Nest

Deep Cut

Haywood's Peak

Wyman / Quoil

sandbar

Ice Fort Cove

WALDEN POND

Fitchburg R.R.

Emerson's Cliff

Pine Hill

Andromeda Ponds

CONCORD
LINCOLN

There had been others along the Walden Road: the Stratton family, whose orchards were in Thoreau's time strangled by advancing pine woods—one of their houses was used as the town Alms House, the other only a cellar-hole where dead dogs and horses were dumped; the Breeds, a family of drunkards who lived on the site of a pre-Revolutionary tavern—when their house burned, Thoreau and the rest of Concord's men ran through the woods with the hand-pumper too late to help; LeGross, an anonymous farmer; and Nutting, who was probably the old man who, in the eighteenth century, shot bear and moose on Fair Haven Ledges and traded their hides for rum.

The railroad workers' shanty town seems to have been in the area of the Deep Cut, although only its ruins were left, overgrown with mullein, as Emerson noted in the spring of 1846.

Nevertheless, Thoreau was far from isolated. Fishermen often came out from the village, men worked along the railroad, "half-witted men from the alms house" passed by, and woodchoppers were busy in every season.

On the morning Thoreau moved in, one of the local vagrants came to the door and asked for a drink. "I knew that rum or something like it was the only drink he loved, but I gave him a dish of warm pond water, which was all I had, nevertheless, which to my astonishment he drank, being used to drinking."

On the second day his sister Sophia arrived to see if he were still alive. Ellery Channing was a frequent visitor, although he lived on the far side of Concord then, as were Edmund Hosmer, Emerson, Bronson Alcott, and occasionally Nathaniel Hawthorne. His friends' families came for picnics—the children when grown remembered how Thoreau demonstrated nature and Indian lore to them. The local women's antislavery group held their annual meeting, with noted speakers and a picnic, before his house to commemorate the freeing of slaves in the West Indies.

The curious often came by, especially "about the first of April, when every body is on the move." He thought the women and children enjoyed themselves more than the men, whose minds dwelled on business. However, there were also the two girls who borrowed his water dipper and tossed it in the pond, a pair of shady men from whom he managed to rescue a young woman, and a variety of snoops and bores.

There came also "one real runaway slave, among the rest, whom I helped to forward toward the north star." (The Thoreaus were active in the underground railroad, but the Walden house's tiny attic and cellar were more traps than sanctuaries.)

Still, Thoreau found ample time for necessary solitude. "I have a great deal of company in my house; especially in the morning, when nobody calls."

Nature

✝✝✝

Nature, to Thoreau, was not a background to human life but a part *of* it; not just raw materials to use and use up, but something so essential to our inner life that an artificial separation (such as civilized technology often causes) brings about a mental, spiritual, and physical weakening.

In addition he had a growing curiosity about specific scientific facts. Being surrounded by unfenced nature during the Walden years seems to have sharpened Thoreau's general appreciation, while the years spent writing his book added greatly to his knowledge. Earlier he had learned the common names of some plants and then forgotten them, but around 1850, he recalled, "I remember gazing with interest at the swamps . . . and wondering if I could ever attain to such familiarity with plants that I should know the species of every twig and leaf in them." When he did "know the species," he found he noticed more of what had always been there before him.

Skunk Cabbage

At about the same time he invented his botany hat, which conveniently left his hands free, although it held only small—and therefore sometimes incomplete—specimens. These he pressed and mounted on large sheets of rag paper with their English and Latin names scrawled in pencil. It is estimated Thoreau thus collected and classified some sixty percent of the species native to his area. He walked miles to visit certain trees simply because he enjoyed being among them, and kept such careful track of some plants' life cycles that he could arrive exactly when their flowers opened.

Although all of the large native mammals were gone from Concord in Thoreau's time (deer, however, have returned in the twentieth century), there were still plenty of birds to observe, and, as with botany, Thoreau's specific interest in them increased while he lived at the pond. "I found myself suddenly neighbor to the birds; not by having imprisoned one, but having caged myself near them."

However, it was not until 1854 that he bought his eight-dollar telescope. It was difficult to focus quickly and nothing like modern bird-watching glasses. Most of his identifications were made by eye alone, and this before any specific system of identifying marks had been developed. A common method of seeing birds close up was to shoot them, as Audubon did, but Thoreau had given up guns, realizing that life and habits were as much or more of the bird as its feathers and bones.

Summer

Loon

Winter

Biography II

Thoreau lived at Walden two years, two months, and two days (July 4, 1845–September 6, 1847). Having extracted what he could from that experience, he next went to care for Emerson's household while the latter lectured in Europe. He then lived in his parents' home until he died. From time to time he made trips—as he had before and during the Walden years—alone or with a friend, to the Maine Woods, Cape Cod, the White Mountains, Canada, and even, later on for his health, Minnesota.

The most far-reaching adventure, perhaps, occurred during his second year at Walden. On his way to the cobbler in July 1846, he was arrested for not paying his poll tax (he had paid all the other taxes). Sam Staples, the tax collector, constable, and jailer, had ignored the nonpayment for three years and even offered to pay the sum ($4.50) if Henry were hard up. But it was a matter of principle—the taxes would go to support slavery—so Thoreau went to jail.

Before the night was over someone, probably his Aunt Maria Thoreau, paid the tax for him. Thoreau was furious, but the essay he wrote from the experience, later known as *Civil Disobedience*, had enormous influence in the twentieth century.

In 1849 his sister Helen died, and his father bought the family's last house on Main Street. Now that graphite was used in electrotyping—a new method of making printing plates—J. Thoreau & Co. provided fine-ground graphite to printers and stopped making pencils. When his father died (also of tuberculosis) in 1859, Thoreau took over the business.

In the meantime, he finished *A Week on the Concord and Merrimack Rivers,* which was begun at Walden, partly as a tribute to his brother John. The Boston firm of James Munroe & Co. agreed to publish it if the author shared expenses. *A Week* came out in 1849 but only 294 copies were sold. By 1853 Thoreau had the remaining 706 in his attic and a debt of $290 plus postage.

Nevertheless, he continued rewriting *Walden* (seven drafts plus additions), sometimes adding incidents that occurred after he left the pond—for the book is not merely a list of facts, but a distillation of experiences. Nor is it a step-by-step guide to better life—rather he hoped his readers "will accept such portions as apply to them." The heart of the book is its philosophy.

Walden was published in 1854 by Ticknor and Fields of Boston on more favorable terms. They printed 2000 copies (twice the *Week*'s edition) and gave the author a fifteen percent royalty on the retail price of one dollar. It sold slowly but steadily, and except for a gap of a few years between the first and second printings, it has never gone out of print; and in fact has been translated into dozens of languages.

Many, though by no means all, Concordians were strongly antislavery, and the Thoreau family, among others, housed and helped escaping slaves making their way northward to Canada. Although Thoreau had written the definitive essay on passive resistance, he admired John Brown and, after the violent raid on Harper's Ferry, spoke out publicly and persuasively for Brown after opinion had turned against him.

By the time the Civil War began, Thoreau had come down with tuberculosis in earnest. He visited Walden Pond for the last time in September 1861, and died the following May.

Afterword

✝✝✝

After Thoreau left his little one-room house, he sold it to
Emerson, who sold it to his gardener, Hugh Whelan, who
moved it some distance away. He intended to add a twelve-
by twenty-five-foot wing and move in with his family, but
when he miscalculated the cellar-hole for the new part, one
end of the house slumped into it. This, his drinking, and an
unhappy marriage proved too much, and Whelan ran away.
The house stayed tipped until 1849, when it was bought
again, and moved across town to the Carlisle Road by ox
cart and used for grain storage. The roof later covered a pig
pen and the rest went to patch a barn.

Thoreau planted rows of white pines for Emerson on the former bean-field. This became one of the more beautiful groves in Concord. After the Civil War an amusement park was built by the railroad track, complete with swings, slides, a bandstand, and an amphitheater suitable for conventions. When it was abandoned, tramps accidentally burned the pavilions one by one with their cooking fires. In 1896 one fire spread through the treetops and burned the white pine grove.

Finally Emerson's heirs willed the land to the public so the Walden of Thoreau and Emerson could continue to exist and be enjoyed. Management of the area has passed through a number of public agencies, some of whom committed obvious violations of the deed's conditions. Current problems of overuse and misuse once again show Walden to be a microcosm of the natural world.

Bibliography

For further reading, some basic books are:

Thoreau, Henry David. *Walden,* in many editions.

———. *The Journal of Henry D. Thoreau,* Bradford Torrey and Francis H. Allen, eds. (New York: Dover Publications Inc., 1962).

Harding, Walter. *The Days of Henry Thoreau* (New York: Alfred A. Knopf, 1967; reprinted by Dover).

Hosmer, Horace. *Remembrances of Concord and the Thoreaus: Letters of Horace Hosmer to Dr. S. A. Jones* (Urbana: University of Illinois Press, 1977).

Meltzer, Milton and Harding, Walter. *A Thoreau Profile* (Concord, Mass.: Thoreau Foundation, Inc., 1962).

Stowell, Robert F. and Howarth, William L., eds. *A Thoreau Gazetteer* (Princeton, N.J.: Princeton University Press, 1970).

Wheeler, Ruth R. *Concord: Climate for Freedom* (Concord, Mass.: The Concord Antiquarian Society, 1967).

I would like especially to thank the people who personally helped me research this book: Ann McGrath and Thomas Blandings of the Thoreau Lyceum, Concord; Roland W. Robbins of Lincoln; Marsha Moss and Joyce Woodman of the Concord Public Library; Andrea Rundgren of the Massachusetts Horticultural Society Library, Boston; and Peter C. Hotton and M. R. Montgomery of the Boston Globe.